How to Draw
POKEMON

LEARN TO DRAW YOUR FAVORITE POKEMON CHARACTERS

JOYDOM COLORING

PIKACHU

1

Start by drawing Pikachu's
head and body.

2

Draw the ears,
and feet.

3

Add details in the ears, draw
circles on the cheeks. Add
fingers and Pikachu's tail.

4

Furthermore create the eyes,
nose and mouth.

5

Finished!

SQUIRTLE

Start by drawing Squirtle's
head and body.

Draw the hands,
and feet.

Create fingers, toes, shell
and squirtle tail.

Draw the eyes, nose, mouth
and detail in shell

Finished!

CHARMANDER

Start by drawing Charmander's head and body.

Draw the hands, and feet.

Create fingers, claws and fire tail.

Furthermore draw the eyes, nose, mouth and detail in fire.

Done!

BULBASAUR

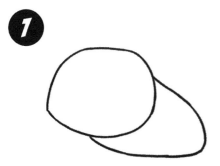

1

Start by drawing Bulbasaur's
head and body.

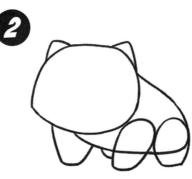

2

Draw the ears,
and feet.

3

Create claws and buds on
the back.

4

Draw the eyes, nose, mouth,
spots, and details in the bud.

5

Finished!

BUTTERFREE

1

Start by drawing the Butterfree's
head and body.

**2**

Draw the hands,
antena and feet.

3

Create wings.

4

Draw the eyes and add
details in the wings.

5

Finished!

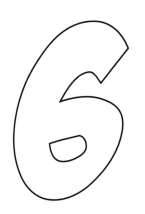

CATERPIE
~~**ARBOK**~~

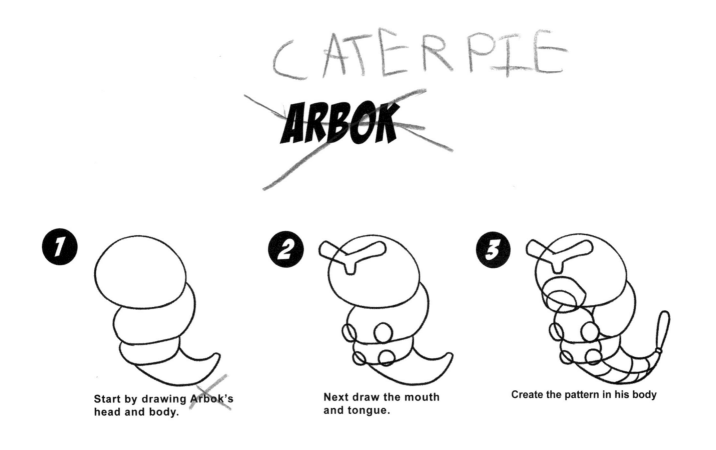

1 Start by drawing ~~Arbok's~~ head and body.

2 Next draw the mouth and tongue.

3 Create the pattern in his body

4 Draw the eyes and details in the pattern.

5 Done!

CHARIZARD

Start by drawing Charizard's
head, neck and body.

Draw the hands
and feet.

Create wings and the fire tail.

Draw the eyes, mouth and details
in the fire tail.

Finished!

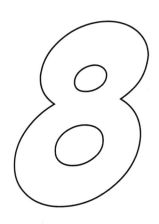

PICHU

1

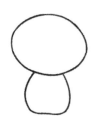

Start by drawing Pichu's head and body.

2

Next draw the ears hands and feet.

3

Draw the tail finger and toes.

4

Draw the eyes, pattern in the chest, details of the ears. Don't forget the ovals on the cheeks.

5

Finished!

JIGGLYPUFF

 1

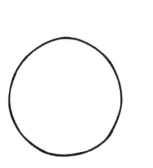

Start by drawing Jigglypuff's head and body.

2

Next draw the hands and feet.

3

Create the hair and ears.

4

Draw the eyes, mouth and add some detail in the ears.

5

Done!

MEOWTH

Start by drawing Meowth's
head and body.

Next draw the hands
and feet.

Create a gold coin in the head.
Draw the whiskers and the tail.

Draw the eyes, mouth and add
some detail in the ears.

Finished!

NIDORAN

1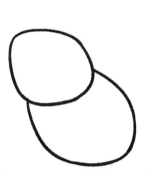

Start by drawing Nidoran's
head and body.

2

Draw the ears,
and feet.

3

Draw the details in ears, claws
and spike in the back.

4

Draw the eyes and claws.

5

Finished!

PIDGEY

1

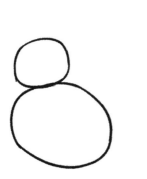

Start by drawing Pidgey's head and body.

2

Draw the hair, wings, and the feet.

3

Create the mouth, feather in wings and chest. Don't forget to draw the tail.

4

Draw the eyes and claws.

5

Done!

ARBOK

1

Start by drawing Arbok's
head and body.

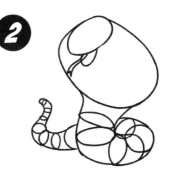

2

Next draw the mouth
and tongue.

3

Create a pattern in his body.

4

Draw the eyes and details
in the pattern.

5

Finished!

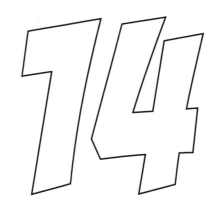

ABRA

 1

Start by drawing Abra's
head and body.

2

Next draw the ears,
hands and feet.

3

Draw the claws in hands
and foots.Don't forget
the tail.

4

Draw the eyes, nose and details
in the chest and tail.

5

Finished!

CACTURNE

Start by drawing Cacturne's
head and body.

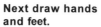

Next draw hands
and feet.

Draw the hat and thorns
on entire body.

Draw the eyes and mouth.

Done!

CELEBI

1

Start by drawing Celebi's
head and body.

2

Next draw the hair,
hands and feet.

3

Draw the claws in Celebis hands
and feet. Don't forget the
wings and the antenna.

4

Draw the eyes, nose and
details in the chest and antenna.

5

Finished!

CHANSEY

1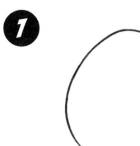

Start by drawing Chansey's head and body.

2

Next draw the ears, hands and feet.

3

Draw the egg and tail.

4

Draw the eyes and mouth.

5

Finished!

CHIKORITA

 1

Start by drawing Chikorita's head and body.

2

Next draw the leaf and the feet

3

Draw the tail, claws on the feet and the thorns on the neck.

 4

Draw the eyes and details in the leaf.

5

Done!

CLEAFABLE

1

Start by drawing Cleafable's head and body.

2

Next draw the ears, hands and feet.

3

Draw the claws in hands and feet. Don't forget the hair, shell and wings.

4

Draw the eyes, and details in the shell and ears.

5

Finished!

CLEAFAIRY

 1

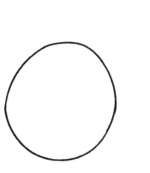

Start by drawing Cleafairy's
head and body.

2

Next draw the ears,
hands and feet.

3

Draw the hairs, shell claws
in hands and feet.

4

Draw the eyes, the details in the
ears and ovals on her cheeks.

5

Finished!

DRAGONITE

1

Start by drawing Dragonite's head and body.

2

Next draw the antennas, mouth, hands and feet.

3

Draw the claws in the hands and feet. Don't forget the tail and wings.

4

Draw the eyes, nose and details in the chest and tail.

5

Done!

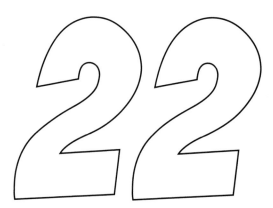

DUGTRIO

1

Start by drawing Dugtrio's head and body.

2

Draw the details in the mound.

3

Draw the detail in mound.

4

Draw the eyes and noses of the trio.

5

Finished!

EEVEE

1

Start by drawing Eevee's
head and body.

2

Next draw the ears,
hands and feet.

3

Draw the hair, fur in neck
and tail.

4

Draw the eyes, nose and mouth. Then
draw the details in the ears and the tail.

5

Finished!

EXEGGUTOR

 1

Start by drawing Exeggutor's head and body.

 **2**

Next draw the leaves, legs and feet.

 **3**

Draw the claws in the feet. Don't forget the details in his feet and body.

 **4**

Draw the canine teeth in each character except the right one.

 **5**

Done!

GASTLY

 1

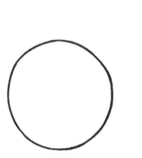

Start by drawing a simple circle which will be Gastly's head and body.

2

Next draw the mouth and teeth.

3

Draw the eyes.

4

Draw the eyes and make a fire around Gastly's body.

5

Finished!

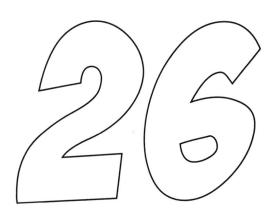

GENGAR

 1

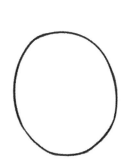

Start by drawing a simple circle which will be Gengar's head and body.

2

Next draw the ears, hands and feet.

3

Draw the hair, claws on the hands and feet.

4

Draw the eyes and Gengar's grinning smile.

5

Finished!

GOLBAT

1

Start by drawing Golbat's
head and body.

2

Next draw the wings
and feet.

3

Draw the ears and details
on the wings.

4

Draw the eyes, mouth
and canines.

5

Done!

GYARADOS

1

Start by drawing Gyarados's head, body and tail.

2

Next draw the mouth, fin and details in the tail.

3

Draw the canines, horn and fins in the cheeks.

4

Draw the eyes, nose and detailing the entire body.

5

Finished!

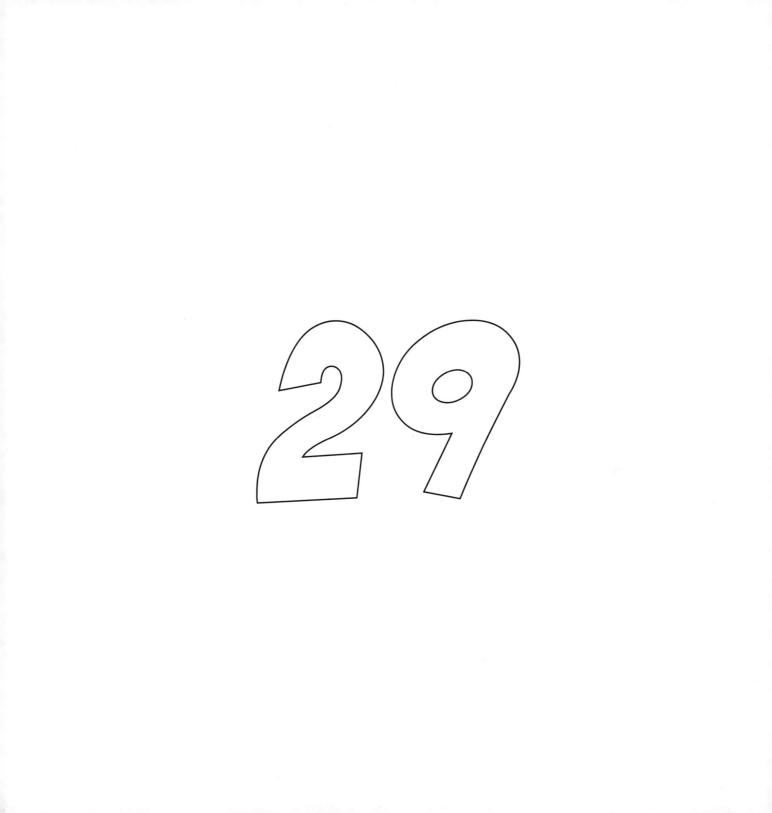

HITMONCHAN

 1

Start by drawing Hitmonchan's
head and body.

 **2**

Next draw the hairs,
hands and feet.

 **3**

Draw the shoulder protector,
boxing gloves and pants.

 **4**

Draw the eyes, mouth and details
in the boxer pants and boxing gloves

 **5**

Finished!

HITMONLEE

 1

Start by drawing Hitmonlee's head and body.

2

Next draw the hands and feet.

3

Draw the fingers in his hands and the claws on the feet.

4

Draw the eyes, details in the hands and feet.

5

Done!

LUXRAY

1

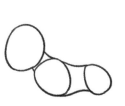

Start by drawing Luxray's head and body.

2

Next draw the ears, hair, fur and feet.

3

Draw the tail and details in the ear, hair, fur and paws.

4

Draw the eyes, nose and details in the feet and body.

5

Finished!

MAGIKARP

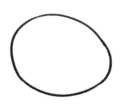

Start by drawing Magikarp's
head and body.

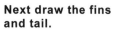

Next draw the fins
and tail.

Finished!

Draw the eyes and fire on the head,
stomach area and tail.

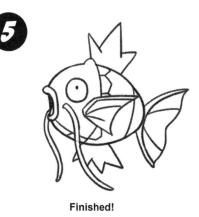

Finished!

MAGMAR

Start by drawing Magmar's head and body.

Next draw the brows, hands and feet.

Draw the mouth, claws in Magmar's hands and feet. Don't forget the tail!

Draw the eyes, fire in head stomach and tail.

Done!

MAROWAK

 1

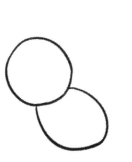

Start by drawing Marowak's
head and body.

 **2**

Next draw the ears,
hands and feet.

 **3**

Draw the bone, claw in hands
and feet. Don't forget the tail.
with the tail too.

 4

Draw the eyes, nose and details in
the chest.

5

Finished!

MEGANIUM

1

Start by drawing Meganium's head and body.

2

Next draw the antennas and feet.

3

Draw the tail, flower on the neck and claws on the feet.

4

Draw the eyes, mouth, nose and details in the flower.

5

Finished!

BEEDRILL

1

Start by drawing Beedrill's head and body.

2

Next draw the hands, feet and antennas.

3

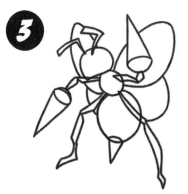

Create wings and stings.

4

Draw the eyes, the details in the wings and the sting hands.

5

Done!

PINSIR

1

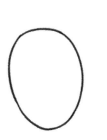

Start by drawing Pinsir's head and body.

2

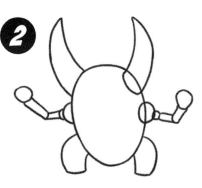

Next draw the Horns, hands and feet.

3

Draw the clawS in his hands and feet. Create some thorns on his horns.

4

Draw the eyes, mouth, teeth and details in the chest and foots.

5

Finished!

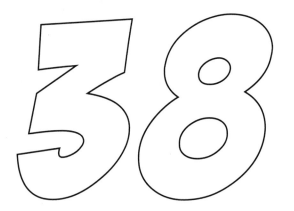

PONYTA

1

Start by drawing Ponyta's head and body.

2

Next draw the ears, mouth and feet.

3

Draw the fire on her head, tail and feet.

4

Draw the eyes, nose and details in the fire.

5

Finished!

SCYTHER

Start by drawing Scyther's
head and body.

Next draw the hair,
mouth and feet.

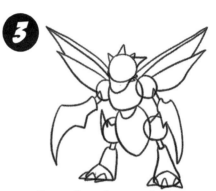

Draw the wings and claws
on feet.

Draw the eyes, nose and details in
the hands, chest and tail.

Done!

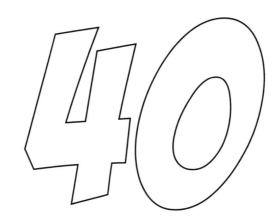

SLOWPOKE

Start by drawing Slowpoke's
head and body.

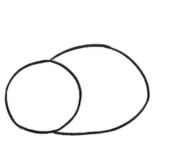

Draw the ears and feet

Draw the mouth, teeth and
the claws on Slowpoke's feet.
And don't forget the tail.

Draw the eyes, nose and details
in the tail.

Finished!

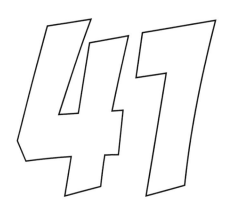

STARYU

Start by drawing Staryu's head and body.

Next draw the hands and feet.

Draw the details on the hands and feet.

Draw the shiny pearl.

Finished!

SUDOWODOO

 1

Start by drawing Sudowodoo's
head and body.

2

Next draw the horn,
hands and feet.

3

Draw the balls on his hands

4

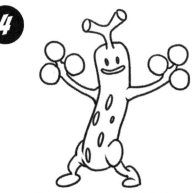

Draw the eyes and details in
the body with elips shaped spots.

5

Done!

TOGEPI

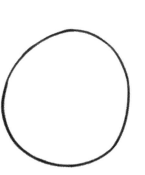

Start by drawing Togepi's head and body.

Next draw the hairs, hands and feet.

Draw the cracked egg and details in the feet.

Draw the eyes, mouth and details in the pattern on the body.

Finished!

VENUSSAUR

1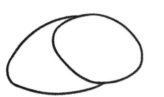

Start by drawing Venusaur's head and body.

2

Next draw the ears and feet.

3

Draw the claws, tree and leaves on the back as well as the leaves on the forehead.

4

Draw the eyes, nose and details in the tree, leafs and spot on body.

5

Finished!

VICTREEBEL

 1

Start by drawing Victreebel's head and body.

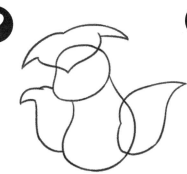 **2**

Next draw the leafs in heads, hands and feet.

 **3**

Draw the sprig and detail in the leafs.

 **4**

Draw the eyes, the teeth and spots on the body.

 **5**

Done!

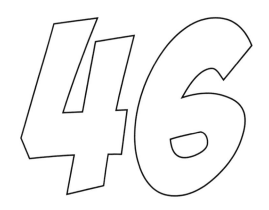

VILEPLUME

1 Start by drawing Vileplume's head and body.

2 Next draw the flower, hands and feet.

3 Draw the detail on flower.

4 Draw the eyes and mouth.

5 Finished!

SNORLAX

 1

Start by drawing Snorlax's
head, neck and body.

 **2**

Draw the hands,
ears and feet.

 **3**

Create claws.

 4

Draw the eyes, mouth and details.

5

Finished!

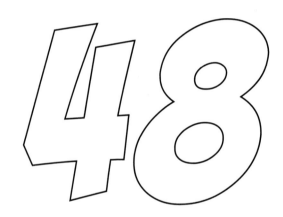

BLASTOISE

 1

Start by drawing Blastoise's
head and body.

2

Draw the hands
and feet.

3

Create claws, shell and canons.

4

Draw the eyes and details in
the shell and cannons.

5

Done!